Profiles of the Presidents

JAMES MONROE

★ ★ ★

Profiles of the Presidents

JAMES MONROE

by Michael Teitelbaum

Content Adviser: John Pearce, Director, James Monroe Museum, Martha Washington College, Fredericksburg, Virginia
Reading Adviser: Dr. Linda D. Labbo, Department of Reading Education, College of Education, The University of Georgia

COMPASS POINT BOOKS MINNEAPOLIS, MINNESOTA

Compass Point Books
3722 West 50th Street, #115
Minneapolis, MN 55410

Visit Compass Point Books on the Internet at *www.compasspointbooks.com*
or e-mail your request to *custserv@compasspointbooks.com*

Photographs ©: Hulton/Archive by Getty Images, cover, 3, 14, 15, 21, 30, 32, 47, 50, 55 (middle left), 55 (right), 56 (top left), 56 (top right), 57, 59 (left); North Wind Picture Archives, 6, 7, 9, 10, 11, 12, 19, 20, 22, 23, 26, 28, 35, 36, 38, 39, 43, 48, 54 (right), 55 (top left), 56 (bottom left), 56 (bottom right); 58 (bottom left); Stock Montage, 8, 13, 24, 31, 54 (left); Courtesy Ash Lawn-Highland, Charlottesville, Virginia, 16 (all), 49, 55 (bottom left); Lee Snider/Corbis, 17; Réunion des Musées Nationaux/Art Resource, N.Y., 18, 25; National Portrait Gallery, Smithsonian Institution/Art Resource, N.Y., 27; Smithsonian American Art Museum, Washington, D.C./Art Resource, N.Y., 29; Courtesy Scott's Bluff National Monument, 33; William A. Bake/Corbis, 37 (top); Corbis, 37 (bottom), 41, 44; Bettmann/Corbis, 40, 45, 58 (top left); University of Rochester Libraries, Rare Books and Special Collections, 58 (right); Texas State Library and Archives Commission, 59 (right).

Editors: E. Russell Primm, Emily J. Dolbear, Melissa McDaniel, and Catherine Neitge
Photo Researcher: Svetlana Zhurkina
Photo Selector: Linda S. Koutris
Designer: The Design Lab
Cartographer: XNR Productions, Inc.

Library of Congress Cataloging-in-Publication Data

Teitelbaum, Michael.
James Monroe / by Michael Teitelbaum.
v. cm.— (Profiles of the presidents)
Includes bibliographical references and index.
Contents: Soldier and statesman—Early years in Virginia—Revolution—A political career begins—Back to Virginia—U.S. Minister to France—Governor of Virginia—Secretary of State—The War of 1812—President Monroe—Monroe's second term—Final years—Glossary—James Monroe's life at a glance— James Monroe's life and times—Understanding James Monroe and his Presidency—The U.S. Presidents.
ISBN 0-7565-0253-5
1. Monroe, James, 1758–1831—Juvenile literature. 2. Presidents—United States—Biography—Juvenile literature. [1. Monroe, James, 1758–1831. 2. Presidents.] I. Title. II. Series.
E372 .T45 2003
973.5'4'092—dc21 2002003034

Printed in the United States of America.

Table of Contents

★ ★ ★

Soldier and Statesman

★ ★ ★

James Monroe lived through many great changes in America. He was a colonist in Virginia. He took part in the Revolutionary War (1775–1783), fighting at the side of General George Washington. When Monroe entered politics, no one was sure exactly what form the new nation would take. He was a key figure during the years when the United States was finding its place in the world.

George Washington with one of his generals during the Revolutionary War

James Monroe was known for his honesty and intelligence.

In everything he did, Monroe was intelligent, capable, and honest. His good friend President Thomas Jefferson once said, "Monroe was so honest that if you turned his soul inside out there would not be a spot on it."

Monroe served his nation selflessly for more than forty years. Again and again during his long career, he proved himself a great **statesman** and a great American.

The Early Years

★ ★ ★

James Monroe was born on April 28, 1758, in Westmoreland County, Virginia. His father, Colonel Spence Monroe, was a farmer and a carpenter. His mother, Elizabeth Jones Monroe, worked on the farm and raised

Monroe grew up in this house in Westmoreland County, Virginia.

James and his three younger brothers and one younger sister.

The Monroes were a middle-class family. Many Virginians farmed, growing tobacco that they sold to the British. Spence Monroe's carpentry skills were also in high demand. The Virginia **colony** was growing and needed many new buildings.

Young James studied at home with a tutor until he was twelve years old. Then he began attending school. He left home early each morning, trekking through a forest to get to school. He carried a rifle and often shot game in the woods. He soon became an excellent shot.

When James was sixteen, he entered the College of William and Mary. The American colonies were on the

Monroe began attending the College of William and Mary when he was sixteen.

road to revolution, however. Because James was so good with a gun, he was soon lured into the colonial army.

By 1763, Great Britain was deep in debt. It had spent huge amounts of money fighting France for control of North America. To raise money, the British began taxing the American colonies. They slapped high taxes on everyday items such as newspapers, glass, and tea. This made the colonists angry. At first they simply refused to buy these items. Then they took even stronger action.

Paul Revere scatters handbills with information about the British.

In 1773, a group of colonists dressed as Indians dumped a British shipment of tea into Boston Harbor. This event became known as the Boston Tea Party. Then, in Lexington, Massachusetts, in April 1775, eight American soldiers were shot by British troops. The American Revolution had begun.

By the next year, eighteen-year-old James Monroe had already risen to the rank of lieutenant in the colonial army. In the fall of 1776, he joined General George Washington in the fight against the British for control of New York. After battles in what are now Manhattan and White Plains, the outnumbered Americans retreated into New Jersey.

The Boston Tea Party

In early December, Washington's army

A famous painting by Emanuel Gottlieb Leutze of Washington crossing the Delaware

crossed the Delaware River into Pennsylvania. Washington knew that he needed a victory to keep his army together.

On Christmas Day, the army crossed the icy Delaware again. Lieutenant James Monroe stood guard that snowy night as men, horses, and cannons were ferried across the river. The army reached Trenton, New Jersey, at dawn. They battled a group of German soldiers hired by the British. It became a stunning victory for the Americans. Monroe was shot during the battle. The wound was serious, but he survived. Monroe was promoted to captain for his bravery.

After a long, difficult winter at Valley Forge in Pennsylvania, Washington's army moved on. By that time, Monroe was ready to lead an army of his own. Washington sent him back to Virginia to round up a group of soldiers to command.

Despite high praise from Washington, Monroe could not find enough men to form an army. He decided to stay in Virginia and study law. There he met a man who would become his lifelong friend.

At the time, Thomas Jefferson, one of the founding fathers of the United States, was governor of Virginia. Jefferson took an instant liking to Monroe. While

A hard winter at Valley Forge

Monroe studied law, he also served as an aide to Jefferson.

When the British attacked Virginia in 1780, Jefferson gave Monroe the rank of colonel in the state militia. Monroe was given the job of creating an express—a horse and rider every 40 miles (64 kilometers)—to carry news between Richmond and the Virginia forces in Carolina. The express created by Monroe was an important way to maintain communication between the governor and the military leaders at the front.

After the war, Monroe joined the Virginia General Assembly, the state **legislature.** There he became close friends with James Madison. Madison was leaving the assembly just as

Thomas Jefferson (shown here) and James Monroe were lifelong friends.

Monroe was beginning his service. Monroe's close friends Jefferson and Madison would both become presidents of the United States before him.

In 1783, Monroe represented Virginia in the Fourth Continental Congress in Annapolis, Maryland. Thomas Jefferson also attended the congress. The members of the congress discussed whether new states should be allowed to join the young nation. Jefferson believed that all new states should be of equal size. Monroe disagreed. He thought the western states should have natural borders formed by rivers and mountains.

James Madison

Monroe decided to go west and look at the land for himself. Monroe's journey was harsh, but exciting. He was impressed by the land's beauty. The trip also

Elizabeth Kortright Monroe

Monroe's first daughter, Eliza

convinced him that he was right—new states should be defined by their natural boundaries.

In 1786, Monroe married Elizabeth Kortright of New York City. He decided it was time to take a break from politics. The couple moved to Fredericksburg, Virginia, where Monroe practiced law. Life was good for Monroe. He had a happy marriage, and he enjoyed his work. On July 27, 1787, his first child, Eliza, was born.

To France and Back

★ ★ ★

In 1789, Monroe moved his family to Charlottesville, Virginia, to be closer to Thomas Jefferson, who lived nearby. By the following year, though, Monroe was tired of small-town life and wanted to return to public service. He ran for the U.S. Senate and was elected. Monroe set off for Philadelphia, Pennsylvania, which was then the capital of the United States.

At this time, the French Revolution was in full swing in Europe. As the French people fought to overthrow their king, some

Monroe's house in Charlottesville

An angry mob storms the Bastille during the French Revolution.

people in the United States took sides. This was the beginning of the development of American political parties.

Those who supported the revolution and the creation of a French **republic** were called Republicans (or Democratic-Republicans). James Monroe and his good friends Thomas Jefferson and James Madison helped form this political party. It later became the Democratic Party we know today. (Today's Republican Party began many years later in 1854.) Those who had stronger connections to Britain and who did not support the French Revolution were called Federalists.

In 1793, France declared war on Britain. The French had helped the Americans during the Revolutionary War.

They expected the United States to help them in their war against Britain. But President George Washington was a Federalist. He supported Britain.

Washington named James Monroe the U.S. **minister** to France. Without telling Monroe, Washington and his minister to England, John Jay, signed a **treaty** with England, promising to support it in the war. This agreement was known as the Jay Treaty.

John Jay signed the treaty promising to help England during the war.

Because Monroe knew nothing about the Jay Treaty, he told the French that the United States would not support England. When the French learned the truth, they were very angry with the U.S. government. At the same time, Washington was unhappy with Monroe. Monroe had given the French his

John Adams was president by the time Monroe returned to the United States.

own view, rather than the official position of the U.S. government. Washington removed Monroe as minister to France and called him home.

Monroe returned to the United States in the summer of 1797. Washington was still angry with him. The new president, John Adams, was also a Federalist, and he did not want Monroe working for him.

Monroe returned to Virginia, where he was warmly welcomed. He was elected governor of Virginia in 1799. Monroe did many great things for that state during his time as governor. Schools were built, and roads were improved. The Potomac and James Rivers were made deeper to allow larger ships to carry goods to and from the state.

The year Monroe was elected governor, Elizabeth gave birth to a son, James Spence. Sadly, the boy died when he was still an infant. This tragedy shook Monroe. He busied himself with work to ease his broken heart. In 1803, the Monroes' third child, Maria, was born.

The state capitol at Richmond, Virginia

During Monroe's first term as governor, the Republican Party gained more power. In 1800, Thomas Jefferson was elected president. Jefferson asked Monroe to return to France to work out an important land deal.

France owned the Louisiana Territory. The French had closed the port of New Orleans, which was very important to U.S. shipping. Jefferson sent Monroe to France to buy the city of New Orleans from the French emperor, Napoléon Bonaparte.

French emperor Napoléon Bonaparte

Napoléon shocked Monroe by offering to sell the United States the entire Louisiana Territory. After much bargaining, Monroe agreed that the United States would pay France $15 million for the territory. The Louisiana Territory stretched from the Mississippi River in the east to the Rocky Mountains in the west. In the north, it reached Canada, and in the south, the Gulf of Mexico. With this single purchase, the United States had doubled in size!

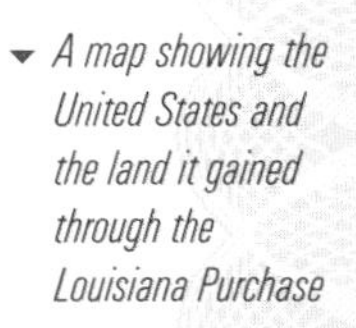

A map showing the United States and the land it gained through the Louisiana Purchase

Secretary of State—and War

★ ★ ★

This time Monroe returned home from France a hero. He was elected to a second term as governor of Virginia.

In 1809, James Madison, was elected president of the United States. In 1811, Madison asked Monroe to be his secretary of state. As secretary of state, Monroe was in charge of the nation's foreign affairs.

President James Madison

This proved to be a difficult job. France and Britain were once again at war, and both sides were attacking

American ships. They took the American crewmen prisoner and then burned American ships.

The British were also forcing American sailors into service on British ships. This was known as impressment. The British claimed that many of their sailors **deserted** to serve on American ships. This was true in some cases. Conditions on British ships were terrible. The food was spoiled, the pay was low, and the ships were filthy. Sailors were treated much better on American ships.

The British also took sailors from American ships who were not British deserters. They needed men to fight their war against France. Capturing Americans gave them

French sailors take over a British ship.

An American sailor is forced into service on a European ship.

a steady stream of soldiers.

British ships often waited just outside New York Harbor. They attacked American ships as soon as they left the harbor. This was more than the Americans could bear.

On June 18, 1812, the United States Congress declared war on Great Britain. The War of 1812 (1812–1814), as it came to be known, had begun.

Early on, the war did not go well for the United States. By 1814, the British had captured Detroit. They were on their way to Washington, D.C., by then the nation's capital.

James Monroe longed to return to the military. He felt frustrated being stuck behind a desk when his country was again at war. The secretary of war, General John Armstrong, told President James Madison that the British would never attack Washington. Trusting Armstrong's advice, Madison made no plans to protect the city.

When the British attacked Washington on August 24, 1814, the Americans had no defense. President Madison and other top government officials fled the city. The British burned the White House, the Capitol, the Navy Yard, and the bridge across the Potomac River. The British then moved on to Baltimore, Maryland.

General John Armstrong, secretary of war

British troops burned Washington, D.C., on August 24, 1814.

Baltimore had much stronger defenses. There, the Americans fought bravely and kept control of the city. When President Madison returned to Washington, Armstrong quit, and the president made Monroe the new secretary of war. Monroe remained secretary of state, holding both posts at the same time.

As secretary of state, Monroe was involved in peace

talks with the British. At the same time, as secretary of war, he was in charge of U.S. military forces and helped plan America's battle strategy.

On December 24, 1814, the United States and Britain signed the Treaty of Ghent, ending the War of 1812. This treaty declared that all land should be returned to the country that owned it before the war. Holding two important posts during wartime exhausted Monroe. President Madison praised him greatly for his tireless efforts. Monroe's greatest triumph, though, was still two years away.

The United States and Britain sign the Treaty of Ghent on December 24, 1814.

President Monroe

★ ★ ★

In 1816, James Monroe ran for president as the **candidate** of the Democratic-Republican Party. He soundly defeated the Federalist candidate—Senator Rufus King of New York. Monroe received 183 electoral votes to King's 34. Monroe's running mate and the new vice president was Daniel D. Tompkins, the governor of New York.

Daniel D. Tompkins ▸

Many people across the United States believed that

the state of Virginia had too much power. Four of the first five presidents, including James Monroe, came from Virginia (Only John Adams did not. He came from Massachusetts). Monroe believed it was important that all states felt as if they were part of the same nation. He chose John Quincy Adams, a northerner and the son of former President Adams, to be his secretary of state.

To encourage a feeling of **unity** among the states, Monroe went on a tour of the nation. It lasted three and a half months. No president before him had done this. Many people thought it was strange and even pointless. But his tour proved to be a great success.

John Quincy Adams

Traveling by boat, horse, carriage, and even on foot, Monroe visited all parts of the young nation. He was welcomed at each stop with big parades and blaring bands. Americans were impressed with the

James Monroe continued to wear the traditional clothes of the 1700s long after others stopped.

no-nonsense man they had elected. They were a bit surprised by how he looked, though.

By 1817, most men had stopped wearing the wigs and **breeches** that were popular in the 1700s. They wore trousers. But the new president kept the old-fashioned look. Though people were puzzled, they liked Monroe and felt hopeful about the nation's future. Many people called the early part of Monroe's presidency "The Era of Good Feeling."

During his travels, Monroe learned much about his country. He saw many Americans moving west in search of affordable land and a new life. He had a great respect for the West and its hardy, rugged citizens.

Americans move west.

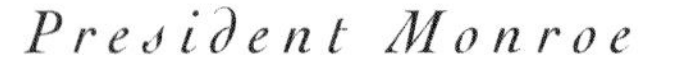

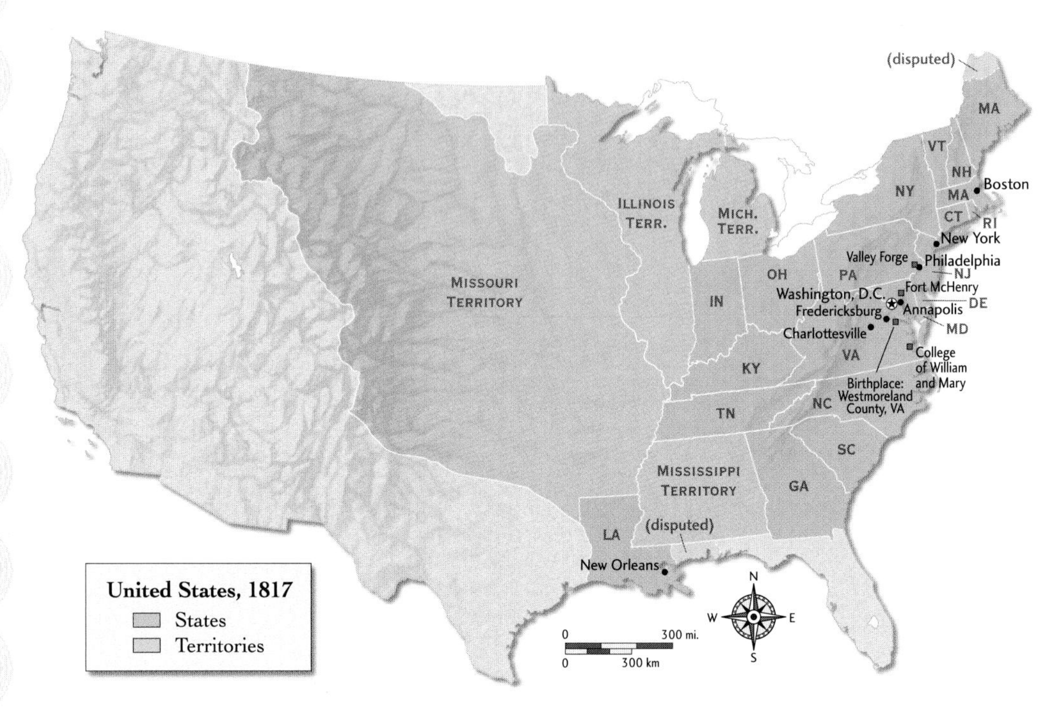

In the fall of 1817, Monroe returned to Washington, D.C., to begin his life in the White House. James and Elizabeth Monroe were much more formal than James and Dolley Madison had been. This bothered some Americans, but European officials were more comfortable with Monroe's style.

When Monroe had worked out the Louisiana Purchase seventeen years earlier, both he and President Thomas Jefferson had hoped that Florida would be part of the deal. It wasn't. Spain still owned Florida. That was causing headaches for the new president and for Georgia, Florida's northern neighbor.

Cattle thieves were slipping across the Florida border into Georgia. There they stole cattle and then hurried back to Florida. Because Florida was not part of the United States, U.S. laws did not apply. Some ranchers and farmers who tried to stop the thieves were murdered. The murderers got away, too.

Georgians were also upset because some runaway slaves escaped into Florida. Native Americans who had

Native Americans sometimes staged ambushes and raids.

been forced from their land by settlers also ended up in Florida. They sometimes staged bloody raids in nearby U.S. states.

By 1818, violence along the Georgia–Florida border was out of hand. Monroe knew he had to do something. He wanted to buy Florida so that it would become part of the United States and therefore subject to U.S. laws. But Spain refused to sell it.

Andrew Jackson attempted to capture Florida by force.

Monroe sent his finest military leader, General Andrew Jackson, to Florida to control the situation. Jackson thought he could use whatever force he needed to bring order to Florida. Monroe had not given him this power, but Jackson used it anyway, and he was harsh.

Jackson stopped the raids by outlaws and Native Americans. He also attacked the Spanish citizens of Florida. "I will capture all of Florida for you in six days,"

Jackson told Monroe. The president did not wish to take Florida by force, but his reckless and hot-tempered general had other ideas.

Jackson captured Spanish towns and forts. He also killed two British captives. Finally, Monroe recalled Jackson. Then he tried to straighten out the mess Jackson had created. It would take three more years of careful talks and some pressure by Secretary of State John Quincy Adams before Spain agreed to give up Florida. Adams finally told the Spanish that if they could not keep order in Florida, then America would. In 1821, Florida became a U.S. territory.

Another major problem Monroe faced during his

The Castillo de San Marcos was a Spanish fort.

Original

Treaty

of Amity, Settlement and Limits

between

the United States of America and His Catholic Majesty

The United States of America and His Catholic Majesty desiring to consolidate on a permanent basis the friendship and good correspondence which happily prevails between the two Parties, have determined to settle and terminate all their differences and pretensions by a Treaty, which shall designate with precision the Limits of their respective bordering territories in North America.

With this intention the President of the United States has furnished with their full Powers John Quincy Adams, Secretary of State of the said United States, and His Catholic Majesty has appointed the Most Excellent Lord Don Luis de Onis, Gonzales, Lopez y Vara, Lord of the town of Rayaces, Perpetual Regidor of the Corporation of the City of Salamanca, Knight Grand Cross of the Royal American Order of Isabella, the Catholick, decorated with the Lys of La Vendée, Knight [illegible] of the Royal and distinguished Spanish Order of Charles the third, Member of the Supreme Assembly of the said Royal Order; of the Council of His Catholic Majesty; his Secretary with exercise of decrees and his Envoy Extraordinary and Minister Plenipotentiary near the United States of America.

And the said Plenipotentiaries after having exchanged their Powers, have agreed upon and concluded the following Articles.

Article 1.

There shall be a firm and inviolable Peace and sincere Friendship between the United States and their Citizens and His Catholic Majesty, his Successors and Subjects without exception of persons or places.

2.

The document that declared Florida a U.S. territory in 1821

presidency was the question of slavery. The original thirteen American colonies had all allowed slavery. However, by the early 1800s, slavery had almost disappeared in the North. The large southern plantations that grew tobacco and cotton depended on slave labor, however.

In 1793, a new invention had increased the need for slaves in the South. Eli Whitney's cotton gin removed the seeds from cotton plants. Before Whitney's invention, this job had been done by hand. It was slow, hard work. Even using slaves, cleaning cotton by hand was too much work to be worth the effort. But once the cotton gin was introduced, more cotton could be grown and sold than ever before. This meant the need for slaves was even greater.

Southern plantations depended on slave laborers to pick cotton.

▲ *Slaves work the first cotton gin.*

When Monroe became president, 10 million black people were slaves. Most northerners were against slavery and wanted it banned. Southerners couldn't imagine a world without it. Slavery threatened to split the nation in two.

In 1819, Missouri wanted to join the nation as a slave state. Northerners objected because they thought slavery should be limited to the South, and Missouri was not really a southern state. They believed that Missouri should be a Free State—one in which slavery was not permitted.

A **compromise** was worked out in which no new slave state could enter the Union unless a Free State was added, too. This became known as the Missouri Compromise. Under the compromise, Missouri was admitted to the Union as a slave state, but slavery was banned in the state's northern areas. Maine, a Free State, was admitted at the same time.

Senator Henry Clay worked hard to support the passage of the Missouri Compromise.

Monroe believed slavery was wrong. But he feared a civil war if slavery were simply outlawed. He supported groups of people who thought that the slaves should be sent to Africa to live in freedom. These groups bought land in Africa and established the nation of Liberia where the former slaves could live. The capital of Liberia was named Monrovia, in honor of President Monroe.

As it turned out, the plan failed. Most of the slaves who were sent to Africa had never lived there. They had been born in the United States. Life in Africa was just too foreign to them.

Monroe worked hard to find an answer to the problem of slavery. He failed, however, as did every other president during the next forty years. The issue would not be laid to rest until the Civil War (1861–1865).

Monrovia, Liberia, was named after President Monroe.

A Second Term

★ ★ ★

In 1820, James Monroe ran for a second term as president. By that time, the Democratic-Republican Party was so powerful that no one ran against Monroe. He captured 231 of the 232 electoral votes. John Quincy Adams got one electoral vote, though he was not even running.

A key issue in Monroe's second term was building new roads. Many people were moving west, and roads were needed to make travel easier for the new settlers. In 1822, Monroe signed a bill to build new roads and repair old ones. The next year, he signed the General Survey Bill into law. This law provided money to plan a system of roads and canals that would open up the country even further.

Another important issue during Monroe's second term was foreign affairs. By 1823, war had spread across

Wagons move along one of Monroe's new roads.

Europe. These wars drew Spain's attention away from its colonies in South America. Many of those colonies took advantage of the situation and declared their independence from Spain. They set up governments similar to the U.S. government. These governments each had elected representatives and a **constitution** spelling out the rights of the people.

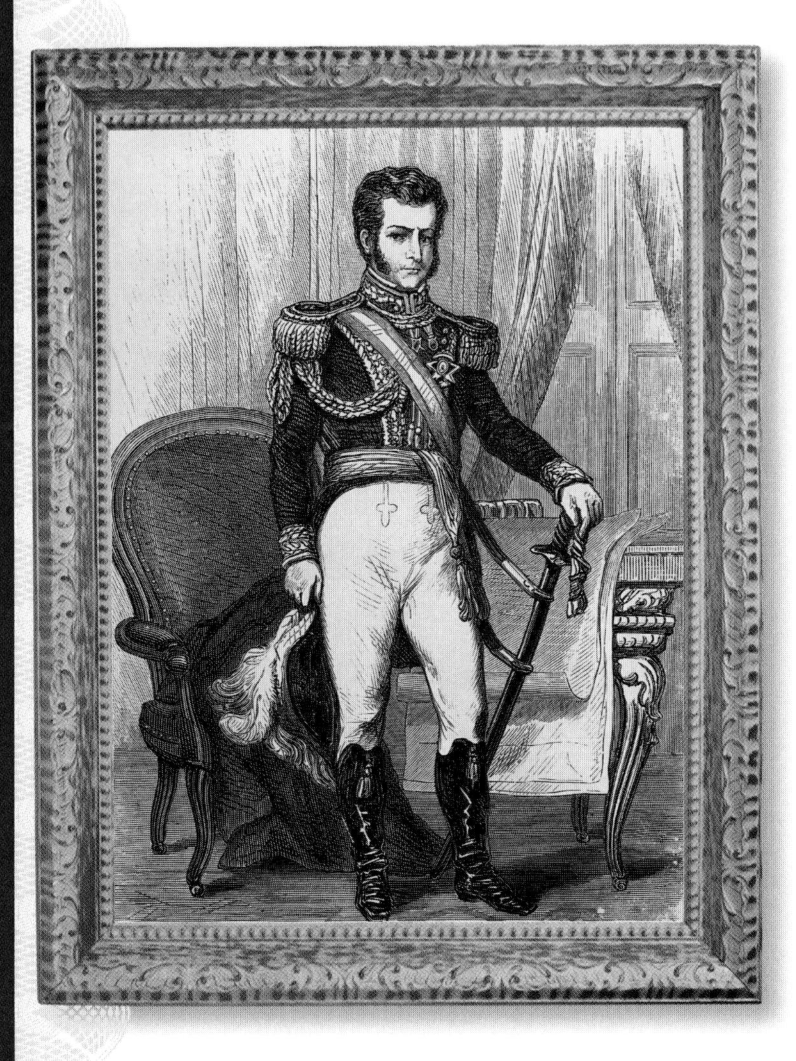

Bernardo O'Higgins ▲ was the Chilean dictator who overthrew Spain's rule of his country.

Because the United States had once been a colony, it supported these newly freed nations. President Monroe worried that Spain might try to regain control of its former colonies. He was also concerned that other European nations might get involved and send soldiers to the Americas.

On December 2, 1823, Monroe spoke before Congress. He declared that the United States would not allow foreign powers to send armies to any country in the Western Hemisphere. In return, Monroe promised that the United States would not get involved in any European wars.

Many Americans agreed with Monroe's policy. But European leaders did not like the United States telling them what they could and could not do. They considered the United States a second-rate world power. It had no permanent army, few people, and nowhere near the wealth of the powerful European nations.

As it turned out, no foreign armies invaded South America. This likely had more to do with Britain telling

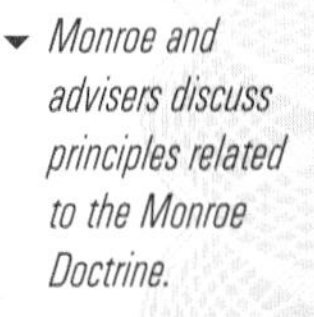

Monroe and advisers discuss principles related to the Monroe Doctrine.

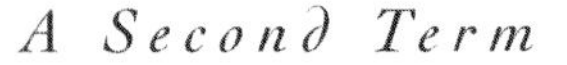

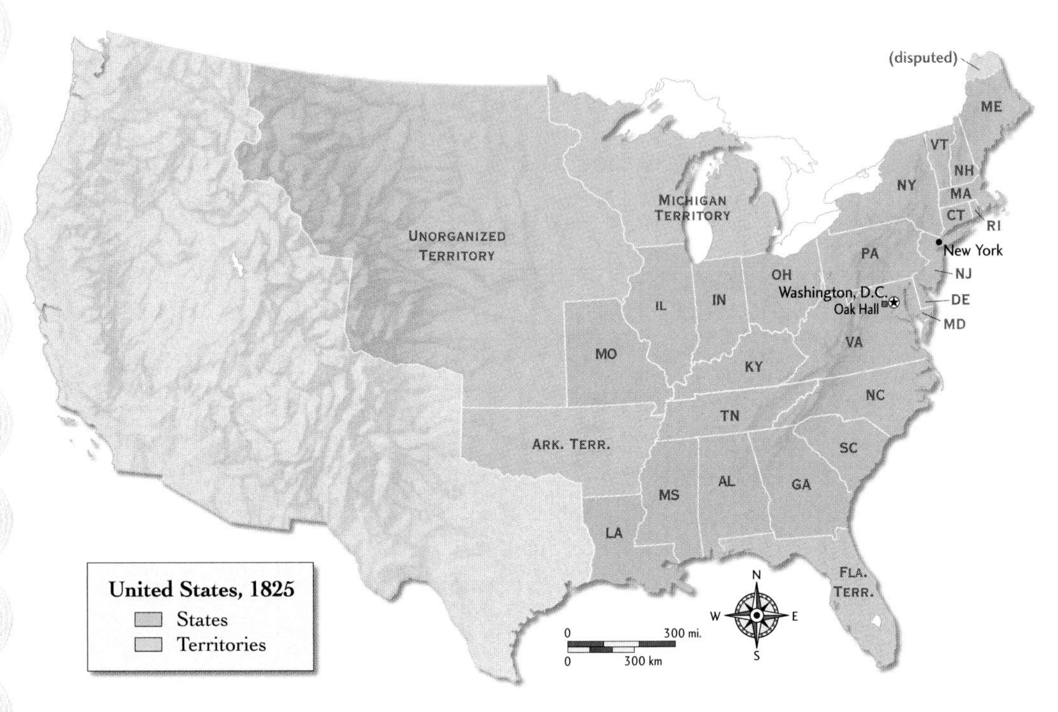

European nations to stay out of the Americas than it did with Monroe's warning. Still, Monroe's speech became known as the Monroe Doctrine. The Monroe Doctrine was an important step in the growth of the United States as a nation. It changed how people around the world—and even in the United States—viewed the nation.

The Final Years

★ ★ ★

Monroe's presidency ended in conflict. He had no desire to run for a third term. He was ready to "return home in peace with my family," as he put it. For the first time in the history of the young nation, there was no clear candidate to take over as president.

Five men wanted the job. Three of them were in Monroe's **cabinet.** Secretary of State John Quincy Adams, Secretary of War John C. Calhoun, and Secretary of the Treasury William Crawford argued constantly. This caused Monroe many problems. The three men were so busy

John C. Calhoun, secretary of war

John Quincy Adams was elected president after Monroe.

bickering and calling one another names that they paid little attention to running the country. They also refused to work with one another, which made Monroe's job even more difficult.

Besides Adams, Calhoun, and Crawford, General Andrew Jackson and Speaker of the House Henry Clay also ran for president. When the election of 1824 finally came, no one received more than 50 percent of the vote.

The House of Representatives chose a winner from the top three vote-getters—Jackson, Adams, and Crawford. John Quincy Adams was finally chosen to be the sixth president of the United States.

Monroe left office in March 1825. He was proud of his years of public service, but happy to be going home to Virginia.

James and Elizabeth Monroe returned to Oak Hill, their house in Leesburg, Virginia, which had been designed by Thomas Jefferson. Monroe had to live very modestly in his great mansion. He had not earned much money during his many years of public service.

Elizabeth Monroe died in September 1830, bringing their long and happy marriage to an end. Monroe left the huge house in Virginia and moved in with his daughter Maria and her husband in New York City.

Maria Hester Monroe

Monroe never got over the death of his wife. His health also started to fail. James Monroe died on July 4, 1831. He was buried in New York City following a huge funeral. In 1858, his body was moved to his native Virginia.

Monroe had helped the nation

grow from a group of colonies into a strong country. Whether serving as a soldier, a cabinet secretary, or president, James Monroe always put the interests of his country above all else.

Mourners pay tribute to Monroe in New York's City Hall, three days after his death.

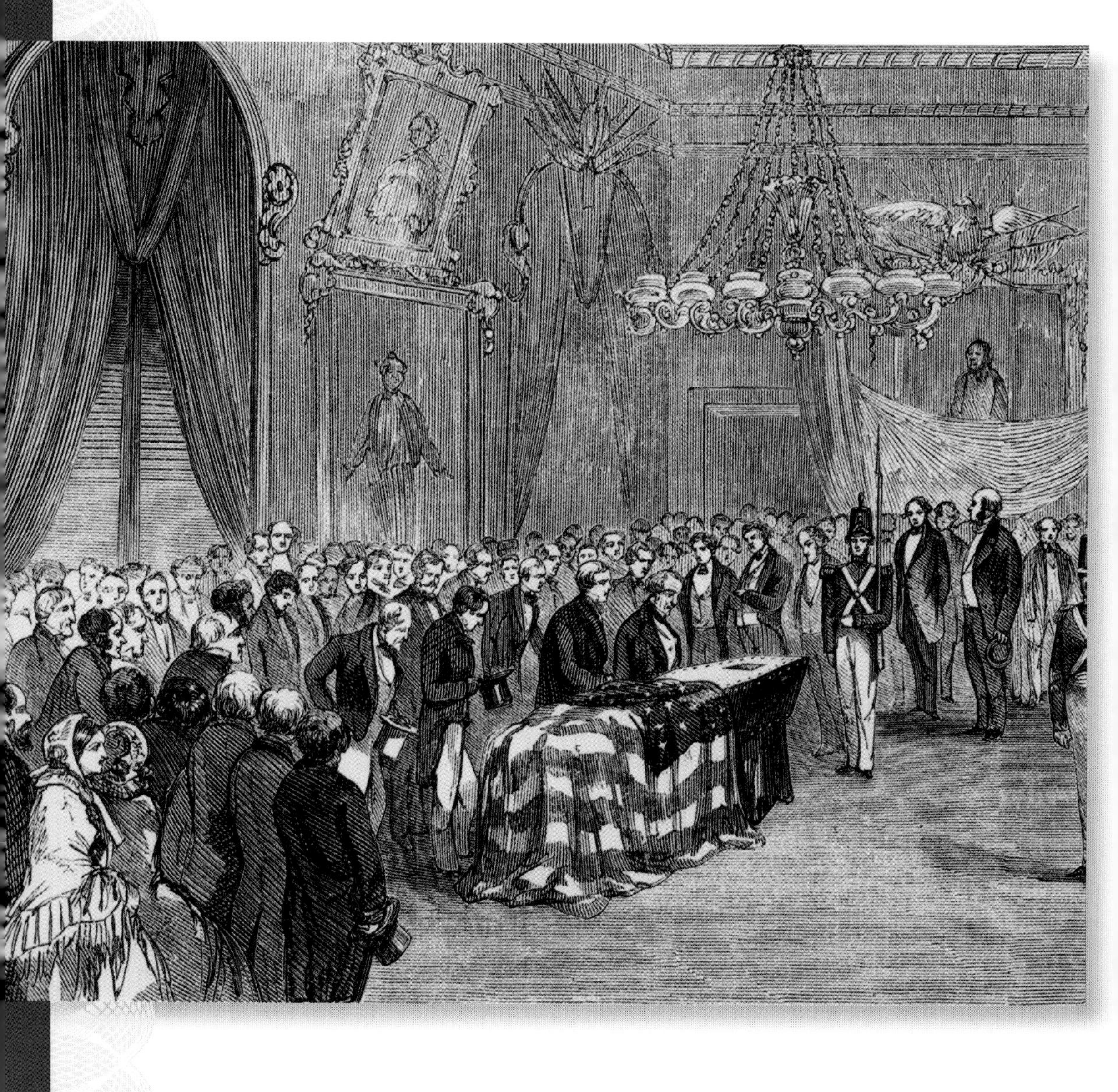

GLOSSARY

★ ★ ★

breeches—knee-length pants

cabinet—a president's group of advisers

candidate—someone running for office in an election

colony—a territory settled by people from another country and ruled by that country

compromise—an agreement that is reached by both sides giving up part of what they want

constitution—a document stating the basic rules of a government

deserted—left a post in the military without permission

legislature—the part of government that makes or changes laws

minister—an official who represents one country in another country

republic—a government in which the head of state is elected by the people

statesman—a wise political leader

treaty—an agreement between two governments

unity—oneness; harmony

JAMES MONROE'S LIFE AT A GLANCE

★ ★ ★

PERSONAL

Nickname:	The Last Cocked Hat; The Era of Good Feeling President
Birth date:	April 28, 1758
Birthplace:	Westmoreland County, Virginia
Father's name:	Colonel Spence Monroe
Mother's name:	Elizabeth Jones Monroe
Education:	Graduated from the College of William and Mary in 1776
Wife's name:	Elizabeth Kortright Monroe
Married:	February 16, 1786
Children:	Eliza Kortright Monroe (1786–1835); James Spence Monroe (1799–1800); Maria Hester Monroe (1803–1850)
Died:	July 4, 1831, in New York City, New York
Buried:	Hollywood Cemetery in Richmond, Virginia

PUBLIC

Occupation before presidency:	Lawyer, politician
Occupation after presidency:	Retired
Military service:	Colonel during the Revolutionary War
Other government positions:	Member of the Virginia Assembly; U.S. senator from Virginia; minister to France; governor of Virginia; secretary of state; secretary of war
Political party:	Democratic-Republican
Vice president:	Daniel D. Tompkins (1817–1825)
Dates in office:	March 4, 1817–March 4, 1825
Presidential opponents:	Senator Rufus King (Federalist), 1816; Unopposed, 1820
Number of votes (Electoral College):	(183 of 217), 1816; (231 of 232), 1820
Writings:	*Writings of James Monroe* (7 vols., 1898–1903)

James Monroe's Cabinet

Secretary of state:
John Quincy Adams (1817–1825)

Secretary of the treasury:
William H. Crawford (1817–1825)

Secretary of war:
John C. Calhoun (1817–1825)

Attorney general:
Richard Rush (1817)
William Wirt (1817–1825)

Secretary of the navy:
Benjamin W. Crowninshield (1817–1818)
Smith Thompson (1819–1823)
Samuel L. Southard (1823–1825)

JAMES MONROE'S LIFE AND TIMES

★ ★ ★

MONROE'S LIFE			WORLD EVENTS
	1750		
		1754–1763	The Seven Years' War (above), known in America as the French and Indian War, is fought; Britain defeats France
April 28, Monroe is born in Westmoreland County, Virginia	1758		
		1759	Author Voltaire of France writes his brilliant tale *Candide*
			The British Museum opens in London
	1760		
		1762	Catherine the Great becomes empress of Russia and rules for thirty-four years

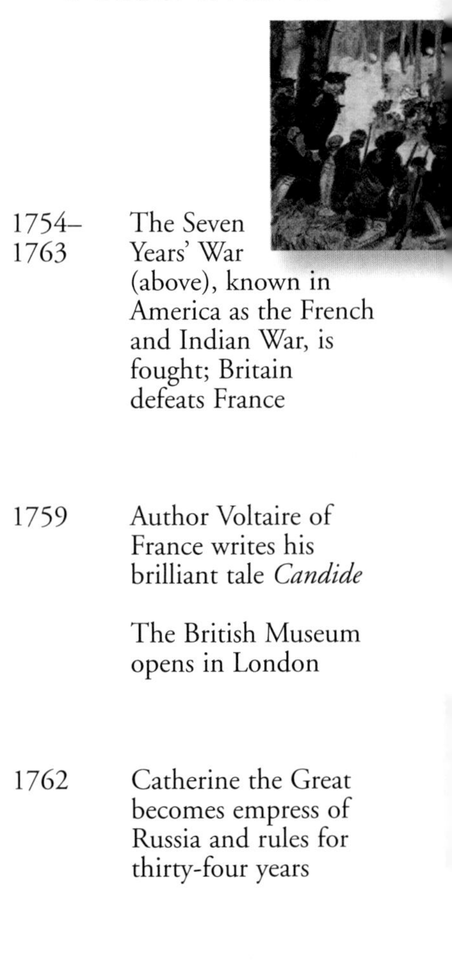

MONROE'S LIFE

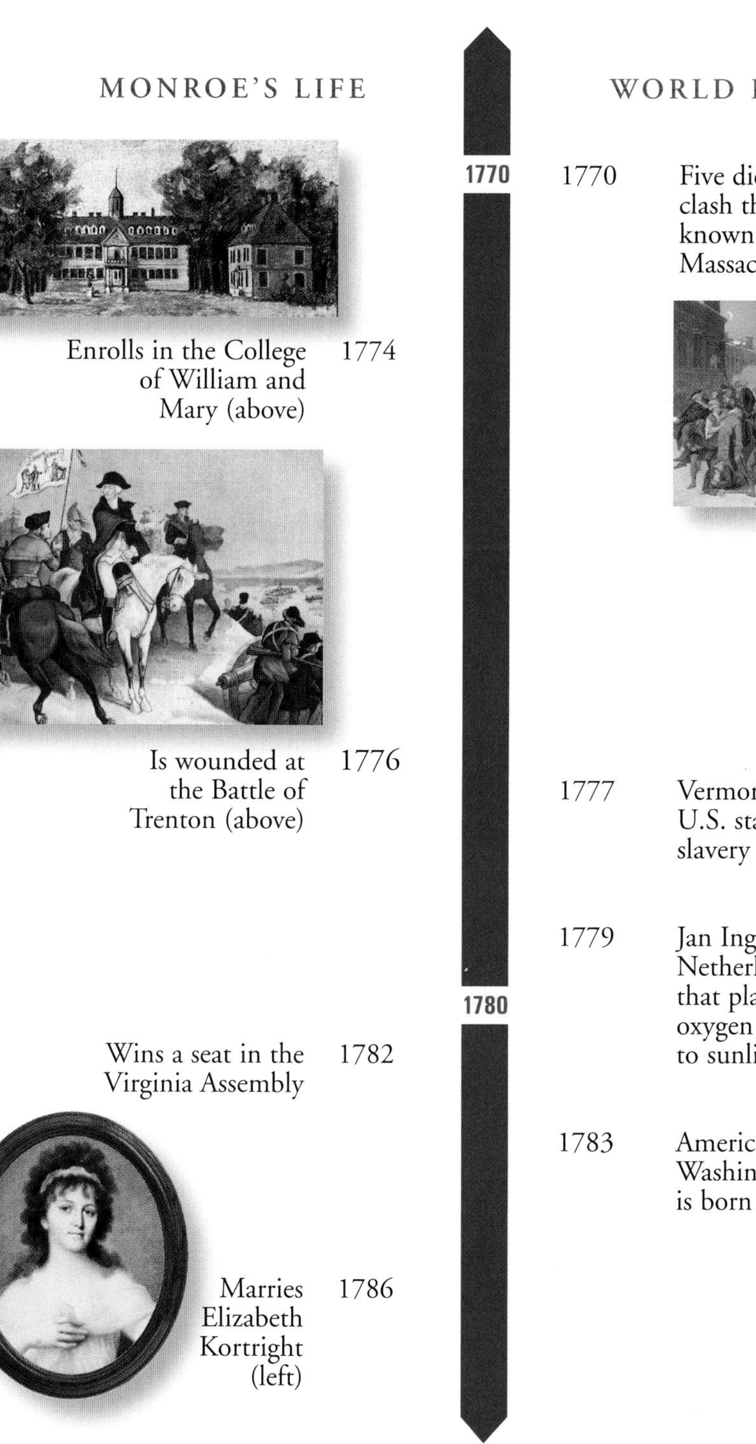

1774 Enrolls in the College of William and Mary (above)

1776 Is wounded at the Battle of Trenton (above)

1782 Wins a seat in the Virginia Assembly

1786 Marries Elizabeth Kortright (left)

WORLD EVENTS

1770 Five die in a street clash that becomes known as the Boston Massacre (below)

1777 Vermont is the first U.S. state to ban slavery

1779 Jan Ingenhousz of the Netherlands discovers that plants release oxygen when exposed to sunlight

1783 American author Washington Irving is born

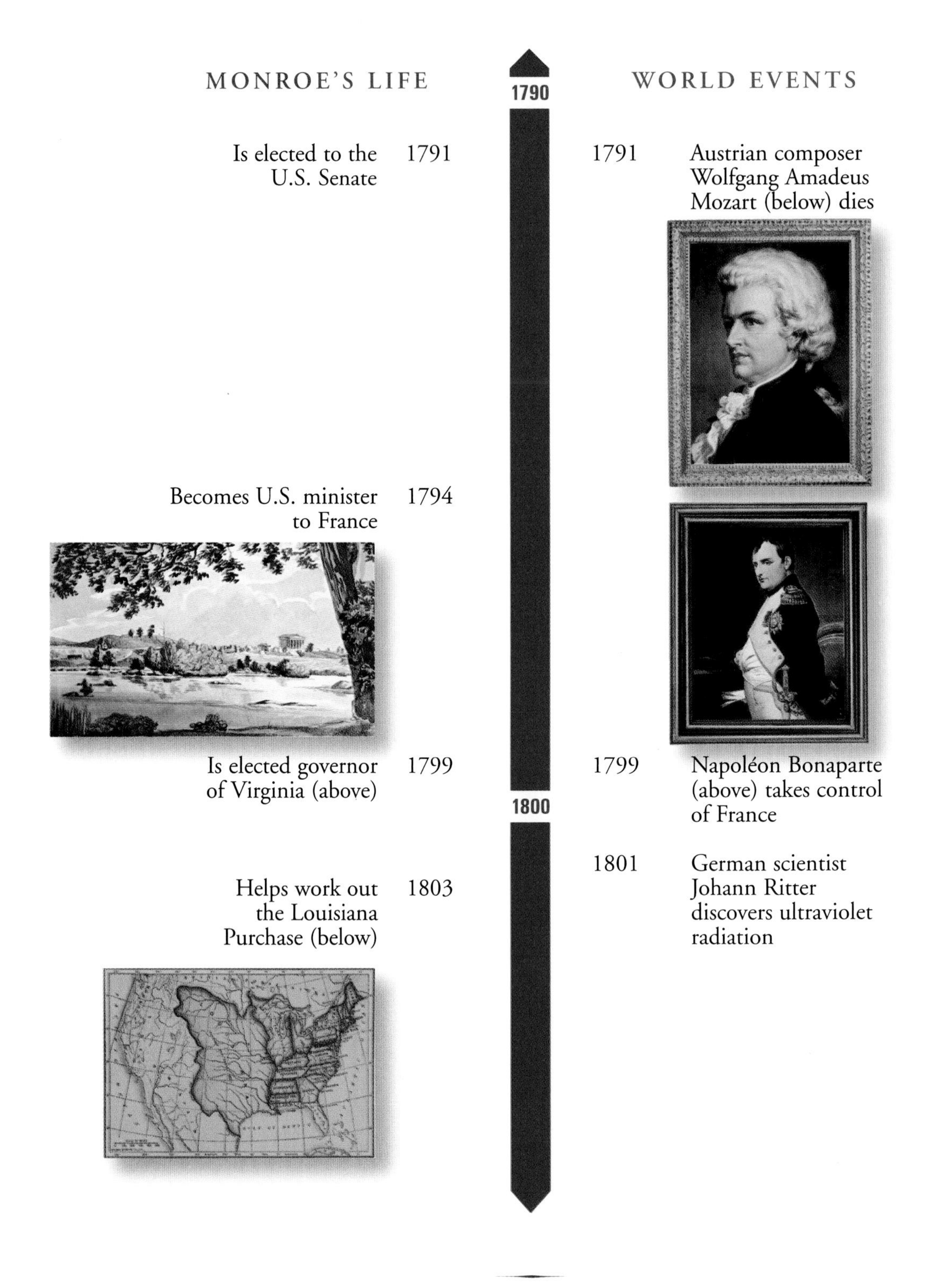

MONROE'S LIFE			WORLD EVENTS
Is elected to the U.S. Senate	1791	1791	Austrian composer Wolfgang Amadeus Mozart (below) dies
Becomes U.S. minister to France	1794		
Is elected governor of Virginia (above)	1799	1799	Napoléon Bonaparte (above) takes control of France
		1801	German scientist Johann Ritter discovers ultraviolet radiation
Helps work out the Louisiana Purchase (below)	1803		

1790

1800

MONROE'S LIFE			WORLD EVENTS	
		1810	1810	Chile fights for its independence from Spain
			1812–1814	The United States and Britain fight the War of 1812 (below)

Presidential Election Results:

		Popular Votes	Electoral Votes
1816	*James Monroe*	*Not Available*	*183*
	Rufus King	*Not Available*	*34*

MONROE'S LIFE			WORLD EVENTS
Is elected president	1816		
The Missouri Compromise, which says that a slave state can enter the Union only if a Free State is also added, is passed	1818		
The United States and Great Britain agree to make the forty-ninth parallel the boundary between the United States and Canada			
The United States takes control of Florida	1819	1819	Electromagnetism is discovered by Danish physicist Hans C. Oersted

MONROE'S LIFE			WORLD EVENTS
Monroe is elected to a second term as president	1820	1820	Susan B. Anthony (below), a leader of the American woman suffrage movement, is born
		1821	Central American countries gain independence from Spain
Announces the Monroe Doctrine, which states that European nations must not interfere in the Western Hemisphere	1823	1823	Mexico becomes a republic
Monroe leaves office; John Quincy Adams (below) becomes president	1825		
		1826	The first photograph is taken by Joseph Niépce, a French physicist
		1827	Modern-day matches are invented by coating the end of a wooden stick with phosphorus
		1829	The first practical sewing machine is invented by French tailor Barthélemy Thimonnier

Presidential Election Results:

		Popular Votes	*Electoral Votes*
1820	*James Monroe*	*Not Available*	*231*
	John Quincy Adams	*Not Available*	*1*

MONROE'S LIFE

Elizabeth Monroe dies 1830

1830

July 4, Monroe dies 1831

WORLD EVENTS

1833 Great Britain abolishes slavery

1836 Texans defeat Mexican troops at San Jacinto after a deadly battle at the Alamo (above).

UNDERSTANDING JAMES MONROE AND HIS PRESIDENCY

★ ★ ★

IN THE LIBRARY

Fitz-Gerald, Christine Maloney. *James Monroe: Fifth President of the United States.* Chicago: Childrens Press, 1987.

Kelley, Brent P. *James Monroe: American Statesman.* Broomall, Pa.: Chelsea House Publishing, 2000.

Old, Wendie C. *James Monroe.* Springfield, N.J.: Enslow Publishers, 1998.

Welsbacher, Anne. *James Monroe.* Minneapolis: Abdo and Daughters, 1998.

ON THE WEB

The White House—James Monroe
http://www.whitehouse.gov/history/presidents/jm5.html
For official information about James Monroe

The American Presidency—James Monroe
http://www.americanpresident.org/kotrain/courses/JMO/JMO_In_Brief.htm
For information and many links about James Monroe

Internet Public Library—James Monroe
http://www.ipl.org/ref/POTUS/jmonroe.html
For basic information about James Monroe and many links

MONROE HISTORIC SITES ACROSS THE COUNTRY

The James Monroe Museum and Memorial Library
908 Charles Street
Fredericksburg, VA 22401-5810
540/654-1103
To see some of James and Elizabeth Monroe's belongings

Ash Lawn-Highland
1000 James Monroe Parkway
Charlottesville, VA 22902
434/293-9539
To tour the home of James Monroe

THE U.S. PRESIDENTS

(Years in Office)

★ ★ ★

1. **George Washington** (March 4, 1789-March 3, 1797)
2. **John Adams** (March 4, 1797-March 3, 1801)
3. **Thomas Jefferson** (March 4, 1801-March 3, 1809)
4. **James Madison** (March 4, 1809-March 3, 1817)
5. James Monroe (March 4, 1817-March 3, 1825)
6. **John Quincy Adams** (March 4, 1825-March 3, 1829)
7. **Andrew Jackson** (March 4, 1829-March 3, 1837)
8. **Martin Van Buren** (March 4, 1837-March 3, 1841)
9. **William Henry Harrison** (March 6, 1841-April 4, 1841)
10. **John Tyler** (April 6, 1841-March 3, 1845)
11. **James K. Polk** (March 4, 1845-March 3, 1849)
12. **Zachary Taylor** (March 5, 1849-July 9, 1850)
13. **Millard Fillmore** (July 10, 1850-March 3, 1853)
14. **Franklin Pierce** (March 4, 1853-March 3, 1857)
15. **James Buchanan** (March 4, 1857-March 3, 1861)
16. **Abraham Lincoln** (March 4, 1861-April 15, 1865)
17. **Andrew Johnson** (April 15, 1865-March 3, 1869)
18. **Ulysses S. Grant** (March 4, 1869-March 3, 1877)
19. **Rutherford B. Hayes** (March 4, 1877-March 3, 1881)
20. **James Garfield** (March 4, 1881-Sept 19, 1881)
21. **Chester Arthur** (Sept 20, 1881-March 3, 1885)
22. **Grover Cleveland** (March 4, 1885-March 3, 1889)
23. **Benjamin Harrison** (March 4, 1889-March 3, 1893)
24. **Grover Cleveland** (March 4, 1893-March 3, 1897)
25. **William McKinley** (March 4, 1897-September 14, 1901)
26. **Theodore Roosevelt** (September 14, 1901-March 3, 1909)
27. **William Howard Taft** (March 4, 1909-March 3, 1913)
28. **Woodrow Wilson** (March 4, 1913-March 3, 1921)
29. **Warren G. Harding** (March 4, 1921-August 2, 1923)
30. **Calvin Coolidge** (August 3, 1923-March 3, 1929)
31. **Herbert Hoover** (March 4, 1929-March 3, 1933)
32. **Franklin D. Roosevelt** (March 4, 1933-April 12, 1945)
33. **Harry S. Truman** (April 12, 1945-January 20, 1953)
34. **Dwight D. Eisenhower** (January 20, 1953-January 20, 1961)
35. **John F. Kennedy** (January 20, 1961-November 22, 1963)
36. **Lyndon B. Johnson** (November 22, 1963-January 20, 1969)
37. **Richard M. Nixon** (January 20, 1969-August 9, 1974)
38. **Gerald R. Ford** (August 9, 1974-January 20, 1977)
39. **James Earl Carter** (January 20, 1977-January 20, 1981)
40. **Ronald Reagan** (January 20, 1981-January 20, 1989)
41. **George H. W. Bush** (January 20, 1989-January 20, 1993)
42. **William Jefferson Clinton** (January 20, 1993-January 20, 2001)
43. **George W. Bush** (January 20, 2001-)

INDEX

ABOUT THE AUTHOR

Michael Teitelbaum has been writing and editing children's books and magazines for more than twenty years. He was editor of *Little League Magazine for Kids* and is the author of a two-volume encyclopedia on the Baseball Hall of Fame. Michael has also written many books based on popular cartoon characters such as Garfield and Batman. He recently adapted the films *Spider-Man* and *Men In Black II* into junior novels. Michael and his wife, Sheleigah, split their time between New York City and their 160-year-old farmhouse in the Catskill Mountains of upstate New York.

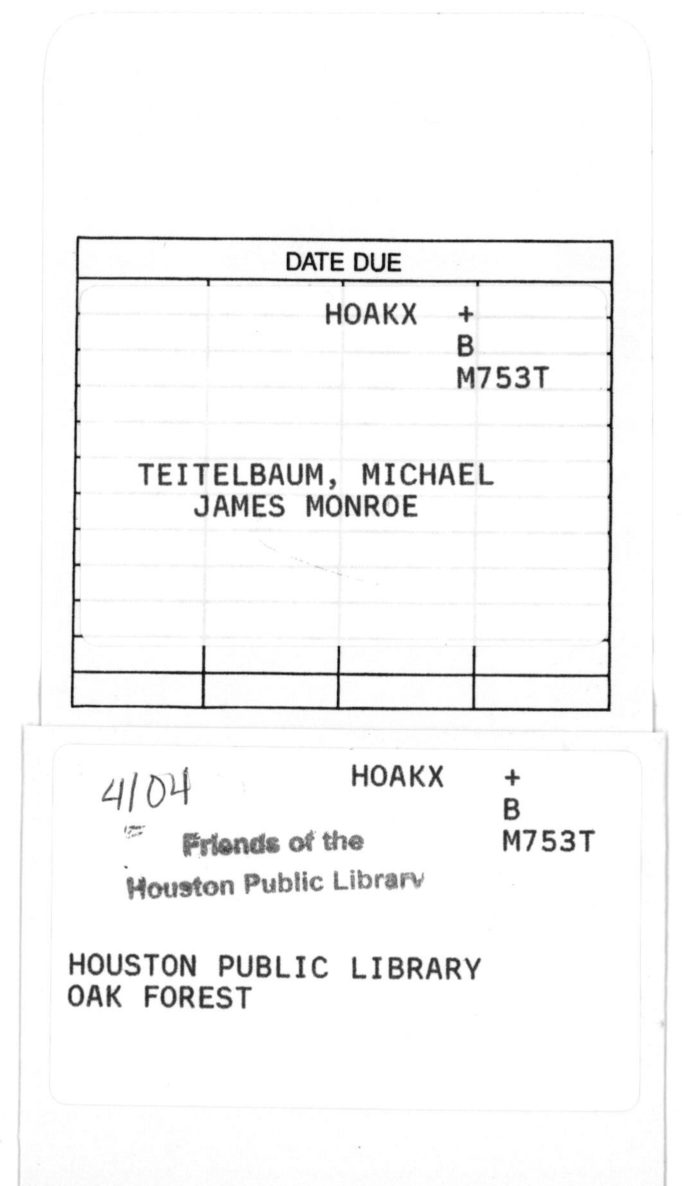
DATE DUE
HOAKX +
B
M753T
TEITELBAUM, MICHAEL
JAMES MONROE
4/04
HOAKX +
B
M753T
Friends of the
Houston Public Library
HOUSTON PUBLIC LIBRARY
OAK FOREST